ANIMAL CROSSING:
Characters

CHERRY LAKE PUBLISHING • ANN ARBOR, MICHIGAN

T0027052

CHERRY LAKE PRESS

Published in the United States of America by Cherry Lake Publishing
Ann Arbor, Michigan
www.cherrylakepublishing.com

Reading Adviser: Beth Walker Gambro, MS, Ed., Reading Consultant, Yorkville, IL

Cherry Lake Press is an imprint of Cherry Lake Publishing Group

Library of Congress Cataloging-in-Publication Data has been filed and is available
at catalog.loc.gov

Cherry Lake Publishing Group would like to acknowledge the work of the
Partnership for 21st Century Learning, a Network of Battelle for Kids. Please
visit http://www.batelleforkids.org/networks/p21 for more information.

Printed in the United States of America
Corporate Graphics

Contents

Chapter 1

Plenty of Personality

Animal Crossing: New Horizons is a game all about settling into a **virtual** life in a small, cozy island community. The setting is relaxing, and there's never any pressure to get things done. But there is still plenty to do in the game, from fishing and

Having a lazy afternoon of bug hunting and wandering around is a perfectly fine goal when playing *Animal Crossing*.

Gaucho pants

880 880 880 880 880

1,040 1,040 1,040 56,6

1,560 1,560 1,560 1,560 1,56

4,240 4,240 1,800 560 560

Total
7,080

If you like putting together fashionable outfits, *Animal Crossing* will give you plenty of ways to experiment. Unlike in real life, everything fits just right!

ch

bug hunting to building furniture and designing your own clothes.

Exploring the island, building up your town, and decorating your home are all a lot of fun. But the game wouldn't be very interesting if your character was all alone on the island. Luckily, there are all kinds of interesting characters to keep you company as you play. The more you play, the more you'll get to know the game's huge cast of colorful personalities. Some might start to seem like close friends. Others might annoy you. Each of the hundreds of characters in *Animal Crossing* has a different look and style. They all have their own interests, likes, and dislikes. Just like in real life, you'll have to learn to make your way and get along with everyone as best you can.

Playing *Animal Crossing* is like stepping into a whole new world. Before long, you'll start looking forward to visiting your virtual friends. They'll help you

Sometimes you might find your animal neighbors chatting with each other as they wander around town.

Animal Crossing is a long-running series made up of many games. Over the years, certain characters have become beloved fan favorites. Some, like Tom Nook or K.K. Slider, have appeared in every game. Others, such as Isabelle, are more recent additions to the series. And sometimes characters from earlier games don't appear in later ones. Each time a new *Animal Crossing* game is released, fans check to see if their favorite characters are making a return. For some, this means a chance to reunite with characters they have known for many years.

reach your goals in the game and help the world feel more alive. The exact combination of characters on your island and the ways you interact with them will be completely unique to you. If you talk to friends who play the game, they might tell you stories about characters you've never seen before. Even if your islands have some characters in common, you might have completely different relationships with them. It all fits in with the spirit of creativity and customization that makes *Animal Crossing* so unique.

Chapter 2

Meet the Main Characters

You'll get introduced to characters as soon as you start a new game in *Animal Crossing: New Horizons*. Timmy and Tommy will introduce you to the game by asking you a few questions. They work for a company called Nook Inc. Their job is to help get you set up in your new island home. They travel to the island with you, and not long after you arrive they

It can be tough to tell Timmy and Tommy apart, especially because they're almost always together!

The outside of Nook's Cranny will be decorated a little differently at different times of the year.

open up a store named Nook's Cranny. The shop sells all kinds of items, from furniture to gardening tools. The things they have in stock will change each day, so check back frequently. Timmy and Tommy will also purchase any items you want to sell. This is a great way to get rid of furniture and clothing you don't like. You can also gather items such as fruit or fish from around the island and sell them at the shop. This is one of the most reliable ways to make money in *Animal Crossing*.

Timmy and Tommy have a boss named Tom Nook. Tom is perhaps the most important non-player character in the game. He will loan you money to build and keep enlarging your home. He also assigns you odd jobs you can do to build up the island or unlock various rewards. Later on, he will be able to help you with big **landscaping** and construction projects on the island. For example, you might want to move buildings around or create ramps and bridges around the island. Many of your goals in the game involve doing things for Tom Nook or finding ways to pay

Tom Nook

Ah! I have some big news too!

Tom Nook drives most of the main action in *Animal Crossing*. He will always point you toward the next step you can take to expand your island.

him back. Any time you aren't sure what to do in the game, go talk to him. He'll always have handy advice.

If you visit the small airport at the southern end of the island, you'll meet Orville and Wilbur. They are named after Orville and Wilbur Wright, the brothers who invented the first motor-powered airplane. These two dodo birds can fly you to other islands. The airport is where you go when you want to visit a friend's island online. You can also get tickets from Tom Nook that let you visit special islands. These islands are filled with everything from bugs and fish to fruit and plants you can bring back to your own island. If you're lucky, you might even meet new villagers you can invite to come live on your island.

As you get settled on the island, many other important characters will start to move in. Blathers is an owl who runs a museum. You'll first hear about him from Tom Nook. Once you've caught a few bugs or fish on the island, Tom will mention that he knows someone who is interested in these kinds of things. Follow Tom's requests and Blathers will soon show up on the island. He wants you to gather wildlife, **fossils**,

Crossing Over

The best-known *Animal Crossing* characters have become mascots for the series. Some of them are instantly recognizable to game fans around the world. They even make appearances in other game series from time to time. For example, you can race as Isabelle in the latest *Mario Kart* game. You can battle as a villager and get a helping hand from Tom Nook in the *Super Smash Bros.* series. Games in the *Monster Hunter* and *Style Savvy* series have offered costumes for players to dress their characters in outfits inspired by *Animal Crossing*. This means you might already know some of the characters before you even start playing *Animal Crossing* yourself!

and artwork for him to put on display. You'll also need to help him build up the museum from a simple tent to a huge building filled with fish tanks, dinosaur skeletons, and much more. When you bring Blathers new items or creatures to display, he will treat you to interesting facts about them. It's fun to try and fill the entire museum. Finding everything will take you a long time, though!

The Able sisters, Mabel and Sable, are hedgehogs who run a clothing store on the island. They won't be there yet when you first move in. But after a few days, you might run into Mabel at Nook's Cranny, the shop run by Timmy and Tommy. After this, she will show up from time to time in the town's central **plaza**. Here, she'll set up a pop-up shop with a few clothing items you can buy. Be sure to support her business by purchasing something. After a couple of visits, Mabel will ask for your help setting up a permanent store on the island. Once you do this, you'll be able to visit the Able Sisters shop anytime you are in the mood for a new look. They get new clothing items in stock every day. You can try on new outfits in the fitting room. The Able sisters will also help you make your own custom clothes and check out what other players have made.

The items on display at Able Sisters are just a few of the many things you'll find in stock each day. Head to the fitting room if you want to see everything that's available.

One of the characters you're likely to see the most is Isabelle, the friendly dog who works in the Resident Services building. She will move in after you help Tom Nook turn the Resident Services tent into a permanent building. After this, she will greet you every time you load the game and let you know if there are any upcoming events on the island. You can also visit her at the Resident Services building, where she offers several important features. For example, she can give

Isabelle

Good morning, everyone!

Isabelle will have a different message for you each time you start the game. She'll talk about events in the village or just mention what she's been up to in her spare time.

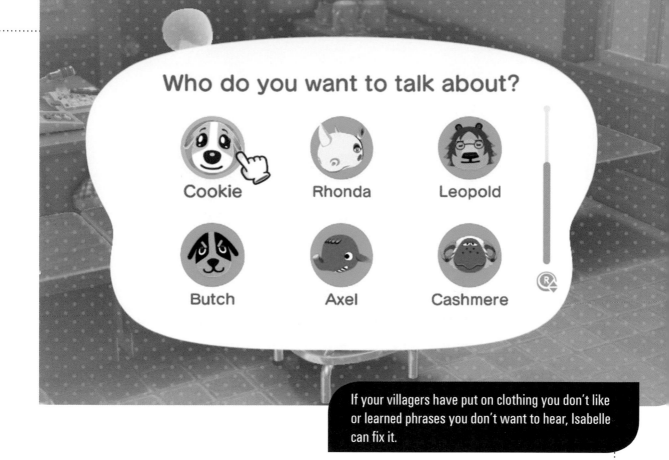

Who do you want to talk about?

Cookie   Rhonda   Leopold

Butch   Axel   Cashmere

If your villagers have put on clothing you don't like or learned phrases you don't want to hear, Isabelle can fix it.

your island an **evaluation** score. This score ranges from one to five stars. It is based on how many villagers live on your island and how many buildings and decorations you've added. Try to get your evaluation as high as you can. You will earn rewards for each increase in stars. Isabelle can also help you change your island's flag design and official song. And if you are having any problems with your neighbors on the island, she can help you solve them.

Chapter 3

Frequent Visitors

S ome characters only visit the island from time to time. That doesn't mean they aren't important, though! Some of them offer valuable services. Others are fun diversions to add variety to your everyday *Animal Crossing* tasks. Sometimes they arrive at specific times or under certain conditions. Other times, they might drop by randomly. Be sure to talk

Label

I'd love it if you showed me an outfit that's outdoorsy.

Completing Label's challenges will require some fashion know-how.

to everyone you see, especially if you've never seen them before.

After you help the Able sisters build their store, you might be surprised to find that they have another sister who sets up shop in the town plaza from time to time. Like Mabel and Sable, Label is very interested in clothes. She will challenge you to come up with certain types of outfits. For example, she might ask you to put on clothes that are "sporty" or "comfy." When she does this, she will also give you a piece of clothing as an example of what she's looking for. Now you need to dress up in an outfit that meets the vibe Label wants to see. Talk to her again to see if she approves. If she does, she will reward you with a unique piece of clothing from her designer label, Labelle. She will also mail you tickets that you can exchange for free clothes at the Able Sisters store. This means talking to Label is a great way to build your wardrobe!

Like Label, Kicks is a character who sometimes sets up a shop in the plaza. This stylish skunk sells shoes, socks, and bags that you can't get anywhere else. He will only start visiting after you've set up the Able Sisters store. Unfortunately, Kicks isn't interested in setting up a permanent store of his own.

This means you should be sure to buy what you want when he shows up. You might not get another chance for a while!

Leif is a sloth who visits the island to sell gardening supplies. He offers a wider variety of seeds than Timmy and Tommy. He is also the only place to get shrub starters, which let you grow bushes on your island. Leif is also a good way to make money. He will purchase weeds from you at twice the price Timmy and Tommy offer. If you regularly pull the weeds that

Saharah

I bring these rugs from my home, which is far, to help you decorate your home, which is near.

Saharah is the best character to talk to if you want to increase your decorating options.

sprout up across the island, you'll probably have a huge pile to sell every time Leif comes around.

Saharah the camel is a visiting **merchant** who specializes in rugs, flooring, and wall coverings for your house. She wanders around the island when she visits, rather than setting up a shop in one location. She offers a much wider variety of home decor than the Nook's Cranny shop. There's a catch, though: You don't get to see what you're buying until after you've bought it! You can choose what kind of item you buy, such as a large or small rug, but the design will be a mystery.

Want to put some priceless works of art in your island's museum? Check the northern coast of your island to see if there is a pirate ship docked. If there is, search around the island to find a pirate fox named Redd. After you meet him the first time, you will simply be able to board his ship whenever he is visiting. Redd sells valuable paintings, statues, and other works of art. You can only buy one piece of art from him each time he visits. You have to be careful, though. Many of the pieces Redd sells are **forgeries**. You'll have to pay careful attention to details and use your knowledge of real-world art to avoid buying fakes. Blathers won't accept forgeries for the museum!

Not all of the island's visitors are there to sell you things. For example, you might spot a spiky, red lizard carrying a net around your island. This is Flick, a wandering bug expert. He will buy bugs from you at a high price. You can also ask him to make you statues of different bugs. In exchange, you'll have to give him a certain number of bugs. He'll get to work and mail you the statue once he's finished.

Flick has a friend named C.J. who also comes to your island in search of local wildlife. Instead of bugs, he is interested in fish. Like Flick, he will pay you a high price for what he wants. He can also make you models of fish that you can use as decorations.

As you explore the beaches of your island, you might spot a seagull lying in the sand. If he is wearing a blue and white sailor's outfit, his name is Gulliver. If he is dressed like a pirate, he is Gullivarr. Both of these birds have the same problem. They have been shipwrecked, and they need to get in touch with their fellow sailors. Falling in the water has damaged their phones, though. You'll need to help them find parts to repair the phones so they can get back to exploring

Seasonal Visitors

Sometimes your island will get unexpected visitors you've never seen before. They are often a part of seasonal events, such as holiday celebrations. For example, Jack is a pumpkin-headed character who shows up around Halloween, while Franklin the turkey visits near Thanksgiving. These characters will almost always ask you to help them prepare for the upcoming holiday. They might need you to gather certain kinds of items, **craft** things, or perform other tasks. You will usually be rewarded with special items that can't be earned any other way, so it's worth joining the celebration!

the seas. Gulliver's phone parts will be buried in the sand along your island's beaches. You'll see spots where water is spouting up from the sand. Use your shovel to dig up the parts and return them to Gulliver. Gullivarr's phone parts are out in the ocean. You'll need to put on a wetsuit and go diving to get them back. Help either one of the gulls and they will send you rare items in the mail later on.

Want to make a lot of Bells as quickly as you can? Every Sunday morning, you'll find a boar named Daisy Mae hanging around on the island. She sells turnips, and her price changes every week. You can buy them from her and then sell them to Timmy and Tommy. The price Timmy and Tommy pay will change every day. If you buy turnips from Daisy Mae at a low price and sell them at a high price, you can make a huge **profit**. It's risky, though. You never know whether the price Timmy and Tommy offer will go up or down. And the turnips will go bad after one week. This makes them completely worthless! Be sure to sell them before this happens, even if you lose money on the deal.

Sometimes there will be a meteor shower at night on your island. When this happens, you will also get to meet Celeste the owl. She is the sister of Blathers, and she loves **astronomy**. She'll teach you how to wish on shooting stars and earn star fragments. These are very rare and valuable crafting materials, so be sure to collect them whenever you can.

Another nighttime visitor is Wisp the ghost. Like the seagull characters who wash up on your island's beaches, Wisp needs help finding items around the island. In this case, he is looking for five pieces of spirit. Simply look around the island for the missing pieces and use your net to grab them. Bring them back to Wisp and you'll get a reward for your troubles.

K.K. Slider is one of the best-known *Animal Crossing* characters. He is a guitar-playing dog. You can buy records of his songs to play on stereo

Everyone in town is sure to show up when K.K. Slider is performing.

equipment in your house. But if you want him to visit the island in person, you'll need to put in a little work. Play along in the game until you get the chance to start doing island evaluations with Isabelle. Once you reach a three-star rating, Tom Nook will call up K.K. and ask him to play a special concert. From then on, K.K. will show up every weekend to play live music.

Chapter 4

Getting to Know Your Neighbors

Not every character in *Animal Crossing* is on the island to provide you with services. There will also be several other villagers on the island who are simply looking to settle down and make a new home. When you first arrive, there will be two other villagers traveling with you. More will move in as you build up the island and complete tasks for Tom Nook.

Musicals.

Anime.

Science fiction.

Something else.

I don't watch movies.

Cookie

What kind of movies do you like to watch, arfer? The world needs to know!

As you get to know your animal neighbors, they will also do their best to get to know you.

Frobert

What? You didn't run an octuple marathon? Ha! I knew you'd bring me if it was something like that!

When you visit villagers at their homes, you'll often find them crafting at workbenches or tidying up.

Eventually, you can have up to 10 fellow residents on the island, in addition to the main characters that are found on every island. That's more than enough to form a busy, bustling community!

There are hundreds and hundreds of possible villagers who can live on your island in *Animal Crossing: New Horizons*. Each one has a different appearance and personality. Some are big into sports and always talk about exercising. Others are lazy, and

you can find them taking naps around the island. You
can't choose which villagers show up on the island. It's
completely random!

Aside from the two villagers you start with, you'll
get three more by following Tom Nook's instructions
and building houses characters can move into. After
that, you will have a little bit more control over who
moves to your town. You will get the chance to set up a

Axel

**You haven't been skipping workouts,
have you? I can always tell.**

Some villagers have bold taste in decorations for
their homes.

Villagers Abroad

Do you play *Animal Crossing* online with friends? You'll have the chance to meet all kinds of new characters when you visit a friend's island. You might even be able to invite some of them back to your own island to become your neighbors. If a friend has a villager that is thinking of leaving the island, you can talk to them and invite them to move to your island instead. Is there a specific villager you'd like to have on your island? A friend might be willing to set up the move for you. This is one of the only ways to pick who comes to your island.

campsite on the island. From then on, random villagers will stop by for vacations. If you like them, you can try to convince them to move in permanently. You can sometimes also find new villagers to invite when you travel to mystery islands from the airport.

The villagers on your island will participate in various seasonal events. You will see them out fishing and catching bugs. Each one has a house that you can visit. It will be decorated to match their personality. You can chat with your neighbors and give them presents. Once you get to know them, they will also give you gifts and ask you questions. It's definitely worth making friends and seeing what kinds of items you get!

If you really don't like one of your villagers, you can convince them to leave. Simply ignore them for a long time. Don't talk to them or give them gifts. After a while, they will approach you and tell you they are thinking about leaving. You can either convince them to stay or tell them to go ahead and leave. The choice is all yours.

Of course, the most important character in *Animal Crossing* is the player. One of the first things you'll get to do when you start up the game is give your

Each time you open a new building or service on the island, everyone will gather for a special celebration.

character a name and choose what they will look like. The name is a permanent choice. However, you can change your look as much as you want as you play *Animal Crossing*. In fact, the game encourages you to experiment and try out new styles frequently. There are so many possible combinations that you will probably never see another player who looks exactly like you.

You'll probably never run out of new characters to meet in *Animal Crossing*. Even if you somehow get to know all of the many villagers in the game, new characters are frequently added. Get out there and start making new friends. You never know who you'll meet next!

Glossary

astronomy (uh-STRAH-nuh-mee) the study of outer space

craft (KRAFT) make or build something

evaluation (ih-val-yoo-AY-shuhn) the process of judging something

fossils (FAH-suhlz) the preserved remains of living things from the distant past

forgeries (FORE-jur-eez) copies of artwork that are meant to fool people into believing they are real

landscaping (LAND-skay-ping) arranging plants and other features to change the look of an outdoor space

merchant (MUR-chuhnt) someone in the business of selling things

plaza (PLAH-zuh) a public space often located in the central area of a town

profit (PRAH-fit) the amount of money gained from a job or investment

virtual (VUR-choo-uhl) existing in a computer program, but not in real life

Find Out More

BOOKS

Cunningham, Kevin. *Video Game Designer*. Ann Arbor, MI: Cherry Lake Publishing, 2016.

Loh-Hagan, Virginia. *Video Games*. Ann Arbor, MI: Cherry Lake Publishing, 2021.

Powell, Marie. *Asking Questions About Video Games*. Ann Arbor, MI: Cherry Lake Publishing, 2016.

WEBSITES

Animal Crossing Wiki
*https://animalcrossing.fandom.com/wiki/Animal_Crossing:
_New_Horizons*
This fan-created site is packed with info about every detail of the *Animal Crossing* games.

Island News — *Animal Crossing: New Horizons*
https://www.animal-crossing.com/new-horizons/news
Keep up to date with the latest official news updates about *Animal Crossing*.

Index

About the Author

Josh Gregory is the author of more than 150 books for kids. He has written about everything from animals to technology to history. A graduate of the University of Missouri–Columbia, he currently lives in Chicago, Illinois.